KABUMBULU CONGO

WILL WILDING

Kabumbulu Congo
Copyright © 2019 by Will Wilding

All rights reserved. No part of this publication may be reproduced, distributed, or transmitted in any form or by any means, including photocopying, recording, or other electronic or mechanical methods, without the prior written permission of the author, except in the case of brief quotations embodied in critical reviews and certain other non-commercial uses permitted by copyright law.

Tellwell Talent
www.tellwell.ca

ISBN
978-1-77370-993-2 (Paperback)

Acknowledgements

Grateful thanks to the following:

Tellwell Inc.: Where would I be without your professional, prompt, and kind services? Professor David Maxwell, Cambridge University, for drawing from his profound studies of Central Africa for a brilliant preface. Echoes of Service for kindnesses and references to the Christian Brethren Archives in Rylands Library, Manchester University, where all the images in this book are kept. Thanks also to Dr. Graham Johnson and to Rupert and Linda Wilson for their valuable photo editing and support. Finally, to my amazing family, which includes my wife, Sheila, who provided many years of encouragement, and our three sons and their spouses, one daughter, and my splendid grandchildren, and for all the hands-on help from Patsy, Ewan, Soleil, Nicolas, Noah, and a host of people in coffee shops, such as Wade, Joanne, Matisse, Yvanna, Emme, Julia, and Andrew—thank you.

Introduction

The photos and stories contained in this publication date from a time before I have clear memories, yet they represent an important part of my life because my parents made these stories and their time as pioneer missionaries in the Belgian Congo a significant defining element of their lives—individually, as a couple, and for our family. Although I was only seven years old when my family left the Belgian Congo and moved to South Africa, the stories, songs, and pictures of the Lubaland left a deep impression on me as a child that has lasted throughout my adult life. I was able to piece together the commentary that accompanies the photos from my own faint memories, from my parents' stories, and, most important, from my father's notes, which he jotted down at various times to summarize his life in the Belgian Congo and which I have the good fortune to retain in my possession today. I was born in the Belgian Congo in 1927, the third child and second son of Robert and Martha Wilding. My two siblings were Margaret (Pearl), born in Belgian Congo in 1923, and Alfred, born in 1925, also in the Belgian Congo. We lived a life that was entirely unique for the first seven years of my life in a small village in what was known as Lubaland in the southeast corner of the huge region that was the Belgian Congo. When it was time for my brother and me to attend full-time school, we moved from this existence to a small town near Cape Town called Fish Hoek. Our life there was quite different from what we had known and experienced in Lubaland. My father made several return trips as he was involved in Bible translation activities. My mother and my siblings and I never returned.

With the widespread interest in events of historical significance, I felt that the contents of this book covering my family's time spent in Central Africa would appeal to a wide range of people from all nations and backgrounds.

My attempt is to also preserve for our immediate family, grandchildren, and their forebears the accomplishments of the people of Lubaland, which included translation work, the building of infrastructure, and the establishment of a large network of medical clinics across many villages. The lives of Robert and Martha Wilding were unique and worthy of preservation in the form of this book.

Preface

Open Brethren missionary work in Africa was pioneered by Frederick Stanley Arnot, who established a chain of missions from the coast of Angola into the interior. He eventually settled in the territory of Lewanika in what is now western Zambia in 1881.

Brethren missions were formed in reaction to the work of established missionary societies and their programs of commerce, civilization, and Christianity. Particular concerns were raised about bloated establishments, churches, and chapel buildings; missionary housing; and the employment of teachers and medical missionaries. Critics demanded simplicity and turned to the Brethren for models of governance out of which the *faith mission* emerged. Missionary societies were to be abandoned in favour of a simpler program of "mission," and much of the bureaucracy of the home organization was to be dismantled and replaced with small committees of wise elders whose main task was to test missionary vocations. The successful were dispatched to the field with little formal training to work under a senior missionary overseer empowered to make decisions based on knowledge of local conditions. Professional fundraising activities were deemed unnecessary because gifts would be supplied through faith in God's provision. Activities linked to commerce and colonial development were to be abandoned in favour of single-minded evangelism conducted by lay preachers, both native and European. The promotion of Western culture with Christianity was to be avoided. Released from direction by home committees, and wholly nondenominational in approach, missionaries were to assimilate themselves to indigenous modes of living. Thus, new faith missions deliberately sought isolated and unfamiliar territory, far from the contaminating influence of European colonialism and preexisting missions, usually called "regions beyond" in missionary literature.

Strongly influenced by David Livingstone, who was a family friend, and keen to distance himself from the impact of European penetration, Arnot moved to Garenganze in Katanga, to be succeeded in 1889 by Dan Crawford. At that time Katanga was indeed remote from direct European influence, located deep in the interior of Africa, almost equidistant between the east and west coasts. It was not, however, untouched by outside forces, and its old kingdoms were destabilized by the activities of Luso-African and Swahili slavers and new trading barons such as Msiri. All of these people had guns, which gave them a great advantage over local societies and led to much violence.

In time, Brethren missionaries did develop their own mission infrastructure, specializing in medical work, which drew in the likes of Martha Wilding. They were also renowned for their work on the production of vernacular scriptures. Dan Crawford made an important translation of the Sanga scriptures; Robert Wilding, along with John Alexander Clarke, devoted many years to the translation of the Old and New Testaments into Luba-Katanga, working closely with the British and Foreign Bible Society. God was introduced to the Luba through the scriptures, and it was important to read the "Good News" in the vernacular. Of course, missionaries worked in Bible translation committees, which were mostly comprised of African members. It was African Christians, converts from traditional religious institutions such as possession cults and secret societies, who made the translations idiomatic, giving the scriptures and important local resonance. Open Brethren missionaries retained their strong emphasis on proclamation of the gospel, and today there are many Brethren communities in Central Africa that far exceed those in the West in terms of size and vibrancy.

Missionaries took many photographs. They hoped that their images, many of which became magic lantern slides, would inspire and educate home audiences, prompting them to send prayers and donations. They also took images for educational purposes or simply because they had an appreciation for African aesthetics. Because missionaries often felt constrained by what they could write for home churches and reference councils, photographs constitute an important source of evidence of their work, showing the full range of their activities, interests, and relationships. Often, photographs place missionaries in situations where we would not expect to find them—with dancers, chiefs, and diviners—a long way from the mission station. And we see their interest in African material culture, craft, sculpture, dress, and body adornment.

Some missionary images will doubtless shock contemporary viewers, and one has to reconstruct the context in which they were taken to understand them. Images of disfigured people were intended to evoke need and encourage donations. They were also meant to demonstrate the value of missionary medicine. Images of animal trophies often offend modern sensibilities. But it has to be remembered that lions, crocodiles, and hippos were dangerous predators that killed humans and destroyed crops and stock. Other images, such as those showing brick-making, might seem odd, but they were common tropes in the genre of missionary photography. Bricks were far more than building blocks; they were associated with wage labour and new types of kilns, and they produced rectangular structures, which were a powerful contrast with the circular structures so prominent in African architecture. Bricks built straight roads and bridges, beat back vegetation, conquered streams and rivers, and kept out animals and insects. They symbolized modern Christianity.

Missionaries were a very different type of expatriate from colonial administrators, prospectors, and traders. They learned local languages and lived in close proximity with African communities, often for decades. They made mistakes and sometimes misread indigenous culture, but the images in this book suggest that they were also able to cultivate friendships—relationships of intimacy and trust—upon which local churches were founded.

David Maxwell
Cambridge

Herein, I will attempt to tell the story of my mother and my father: two beautiful rivers that eventually flowed into one, bringing healing, hope, and salvation to thousands.

First, my father's story.

My father, Robert James Wilding, was born at 42 Hawkstone Street in the district of Toxeth, Liverpool, on September 27, 1888. The district was and still is named the "Dingle," for most of the men who lived there were dock workers as it was located beside the river. His father was Charles Robert and his mother, Isabella Wilding (née Harvey). My father's original birth certificate is in my collection, and I have attached a copy here.

Interestingly, there were some famous people born in the Dingle, including the Beatles!

As of the date of publication, I have not been able to track down any information on my grandparents, other than what appears on the birth certificate and some details handed down orally through the years. I do, however, have a vast collection of letters, documents, and articles that belonged to my dad, which have helped me tell his story.

My grandparents had three sons: Oliver was the eldest, then came Alf, followed by my father, Robert. Charles passed away when Dad was a teenager. The passing of my grandfather brought much distress to my grandmother and her three sons. In October 1905, my dad volunteered for the Royal Navy. He was seventeen years old. As documented on his Naval Record, he commenced service on his eighteenth birthday. He served fully with the Royal Navy for twelve years.

My father's older brother Oliver married but had no children. I wish I had more information about him. His brother Alf married and had a son and two daughters. As a boy, I met my three cousins, but unfortunately, after our return to Africa, the son was involved in a serious accident where he fell from a roof while trying to recover a soccer ball and died as a result. We had no further contact with my remaining cousins, our being so far away in Africa.

I have included some copies of my father's handwritten notes about his life. You will see that he lists his christening, confirmation, and communion in the Church of England. His family was quite religious, and I remember my father would often sing the liturgy and its refrain: "Holy, holy, Lord God of Hosts." But my dad's most sacred memory was his conversion experience during the Welsh Revival under Evan Roberts. It was 1905, and he was in the Navy. He remained committed to Jesus Christ throughout his life. And what a life it was!

While he was in the Navy, my grandmother married a Mr. Cleary from Ireland, and they had a son named John, who became a stepbrother to Dad. I never met his mother or stepfather. They both passed away while Dad was in the Congo on his first missionary trip.

John used to tell us that when he was a kid, he would hear my dad praying for him at night. This would have been during times that my dad was on leave from the Navy. My uncle John and his wife, Aunt Margaret, became very close with my parents and stood by Mum and Dad throughout the tough years in the Congo, some of which coincided with the Great Depression. John and Margaret had two daughters: Sylvia and Joyce. Our families spent a lot of time together.

Life In The Navy And Early Influences Robert James Wilding

I will now attempt to piece together a bit about my dad's service in the Royal Navy. As I mentioned earlier, after his father's passing, it was agreed that my dad would join the Navy. He commenced his service in 1905 and served on several ships until 1912. The ships he served on were as follows:

HMS *BOSCAWEN III*   OCT. 2, 1905, TO JAN. 6, 1906

This coincided with my father's conversion during the Welsh Revival, when thousands of people, mostly in Wales and the west of England, made a new commitment to Christ. The movement had worldwide impact. Before leaving for service on the ships listed below, my father was in great demand as a speaker in Brethren churches in such places as Plymouth, Portsmouth, Exeter, Totnes, and Bridford Mills. He formed many deep friendships during this time, and many of these people would stand behind him and Mum in future years in the Congo.)

HMS *BOSCAWEN III*	JAN. 9, 1906, TO JAN. 31, 1906
HMS *HAWKE*	FEB. 1 TO MAY 6, 1906
HMS *VIVID*	MAY 12 TO MAY 21, 1906
HMS *EUROPA*	JUNE 1 TO JUNE 21, 1906
HMS *VIVID*	JUNE 22 TO JULY 23, 1906
HMS *TERRIBLE*	JULY 24 TO SEPT. 18, 1906
HMS *PROMETHEUS*	SEPT. 19 TO SEPT. 26, 1906
HMS *PROMETHEUS*	SEPT. 27, 1906, TO JULY 4, 1907
HMS *PROMETHEUS*	JULY 5, 1907, TO SEPT. 30, 1907

HMS *GIBRALTER*	OCT. 1, 1908, TO DEC. 19, 1908
HMS *VIVID*	DEC. 20, 1908, TO MAR. 3, 1910
HMS *EAGLE*	MAR. 4, 1910, TO OCT. 3, 1910
HMS *GLOUCESTER*	SEPT. 4, 1910, TO OCT. 29, 1912 (Shore by purchase—a miracle, indeed!)

In October 1905, at the age of seventeen, my father boarded the famous old B*oscawen III*, which was then serving as a training ship. While he enlisted to serve his country, he was so deeply challenged by his newfound understanding of Jesus and the power of prayer that he spent as much time in prayer as possible, often on his knees. One day a fellow sailor saw him praying and quietly said to him, "Say one for me." This would be the beginning of my father sharing his faith throughout his Navy years.

In 1906, my father joined the crew of the HMS *Hawke*. The following two years spent aboard a number of different ships were to be some of the most exciting yet challenging years of his life. The HMS *Hawke* sailed off for China, going around the Cape of Good Hope and stopping in Simon's Town—the British naval base near Cape Town—before rounding the continent of Africa, where he was later to spend many years, unbeknownst to him at the time.

The ship then proceeded to sail to Hong Kong. At this time, Hong Kong was still a British colony, a status it had held since the end of the first opium war in 1842. During the voyage to China, Dad read a book about Dr. David Livingstone—his explorations and missionary work in Central Africa. Livingstone's story had a tremendous influence on my dad and his desire to serve God.

Although I don't have much information from the time Dad was in China, he undoubtedly had contact with missionaries there. The valiant Hudson Taylor, who went as a pioneer to China in 1832, passed away in 1905, just before Dad would have arrived, but I believe there were well over 100 mission stations that Taylor had set up across the country. This was an absolutely remarkable work of God. The story of His redeeming grace in China had a deep effect on my dad, as did Livingstone's work. As I reflect on these God-ordained events in my father's life, I see the Lord graciously and powerfully preparing Dad for Congo and the challenges that lay ahead.

While my dad's ship (which could be one of three or four in his service record from 1906) was tied up in Hong Kong, a typhoon suddenly struck. This was a very powerful typhoon that caused vast damage and left thousands killed or wounded. Dad's ship was being severely rocked about while many smaller boats were sinking. Dad gathered a few sailors to pray for deliverance, and he prayed his own personal prayer: "Lord, if You bring me out of this alive, I will go to Africa as a missionary." They were spared death—and Dad kept his word. He always referred to this as his final call and consecration.

After China, it was off to Australia. This voyage would have taken place aboard one of the ships on which he served between 1906 and September 1908. Some of these ships are pictured. Just looking at these pictures takes me back to an era I never knew but that I can vividly imagine.

My father's experience in Sydney would have an immediate and lifelong effect on him. Either he had previously arranged contacts with Christian friends in the city, or he found his way to a Brethren church there, but he was warmly taken in by the people of the church. A woman by the name of Nellie Sloan, her mother, and her siblings became like his second family while he was in Sydney, and this family would go on to be spiritual and financial partners of my parents through the Africa years and beyond. I believe the father had passed away. Having travelled all the way across the world, this family was a gift to my father during his days in Australia. Many years later, Mum and Dad entertained sailors from the naval base near Fish Hoek, South Africa, in a similar way.

Although Dad had been christened as a baby, the Australian believers were delighted when he asked if he could be baptized—a joyous event that took place in 1906. It could have been a beach baptism. In the Congo, in future years, Dad would be the one to baptize native believers in the Lualaba River.

There were undoubtedly many opportunities for preaching the gospel in and around Sydney, including open-air services. Sydney has through the years been a city comprised of strong evangelical churches, including the Church of England (the Anglican Church). Many, many missionaries embarked on missions around the world from Australia. One of them came as a nurse to help my mum while we were in the Congo. Her name was Margaret Morton, the mother of our dear friend Marguerite Green (wife of Kiwi Green).

The next series of stops would be perhaps the most challenging and influential in terms of preparing my father for the primitive conditions he and my mum would endure in the Congo. He was now sailing between the islands of the South Seas, every one of which had populations that practised cannibalism. Dad was well read in the stories of the missionaries, as I will touch on in the next several paragraphs.

His first island visit was to the New Hebrides, where the well-known veteran missionary John G. Paton had arrived with his wife in 1839 from Scotland and, after surviving multiple attacks by cannibals, finally passed away at the age of eighty-three. Many missionaries joined Paton, and many natives turned to Christ and churches were formed. But there was a high price to pay as missionaries ran the risk of being killed and eaten.

John Geddie, a Scottish-Canadian Presbyterian, was perhaps the first Christian missionary to arrive in the New Hebrides with his wife in 1815. He died in 1872. Geddie faced all the horrors of doing missionary work among cannibals but lived a fulfilling life on the island with his wife. As did Paton, he visited several adjoining islands during his time in the South Seas and died on the island of Aneityum. While he was still alive, he recorded the killing and cannibalism of twenty-two British sailors from the HMS *Sovereign*. Geddie became known as the father of the Presbyterian missions in the South Seas.

There are hundreds of South Sea islands, from Loyalty to Tahiti to the Cook Islands, Fiji, New Caledonia, and on and on until you reach Erronmanga, New Hebrides. They are small, but the area they encompass is vast. To try to get one's head around the scope of the Christian mission over this vast region of scattered islands and people is very difficult!

John Williams was a man with a vision to preach the gospel of Christ, not just to one island but to all of the South Seas. Sent out to the Society Islands in 1817 by the London Missionary Society, his vigour and vision was so great that he became known as the Apostle of the South Seas. After outstanding outpourings of the Spirit in such places, he sailed off to New Hebrides in one of his own boats with native Christian teachers accompanying him. Before they even landed in Erromango, the ferocious cannibals dragged Williams and some of the others ashore, clubbed them to death, and ate them. Williams' story is fascinating, and you can read more about his life and missionary work in Robert Glovers' marvellous book *The Progress of Modern Missions* or on the Internet.

There were many other martyrs for Christ in those islands. May God bless them and their families.

Dad spoke and wrote about his call from God to go to Africa being loudest in the last weeks he spent in the South Seas. It was now time for his term of service in the South Seas to end. All the way back to England, his prayer was, "Lord, lead me and cause a miracle to happen allowing me to leave the Navy short of my term." His ship (probably the HMS *Prometheus*) arrived in England in October 1908.

I will now move on to a very different era in my dad's life—that of the young sailor arriving in Central Africa. This is where he would begin a whole new life with his future wife, who all this time had been doing God's work on the other side of the world.

Here are the lyrics to one of dad's favourite hymns. You can see from his handwritten copy of it that it really touched a chord with him, and when he sang it, the words came from his heart.

"The Personal Call" by Mrs. R. A. Jarvie (arranged by Will Gardner-Hunter)

I cannot stay for Jesus calls,
No, I must haste away,
To join the ranks of those beneath the cross of Calvary.
I've heard Him call so oft before
But Satan held me fast.
I do not trifle anymore, this call may be the last.
I wonder how I could withhold
My life so long from Him,
And join the foe against my Lord, it makes my eyes grow dim.
T'was wonderous love that made Him wait
T'was mighty matchless grace.
But now I go to serve with Him, it is my rightful place.
Oh, could you get one little glimpse
Of what your ransom cost,
You would not stay one other day with Satan and his host.
I'm going now for Jesus calls,
My captain and my guide.
And cost the battle what it may, I'm on the winning side.
Oh, come and be a soldier too
And do a soldier's share,
The captain is the Lord Himself, the field is everywhere.

One of my father's joys on his return to the UK and the home fleet was seeing one of his fellow sailors turn his life over to Christ in early 1910. This sailor's name was Albert Abrahams, and he, along with his wife, would become lifelong friends of Mum and Dad's. Albert Abrahams would go on to teach scripture in the UK and elsewhere, and he and his wife were incredible sources of strength and encouragement for my parents in the long years spent in the Congo.

In 1910, Dad served on the HMS *Eagle*, followed by the HMS *Gloucester*, on which he served until 1912. This was part of the home fleet, which, in the latter part of this period, assembled with other North Atlantic–based ships in Scapa Flow in Northeast Scotland. There were ominous signs of trouble ahead.

The German Empire had pretty well overtaken the British industrial complex and was building its military strength, which included more naval ships. My father could not have faced a more difficult scenario as he prepared to make a request to leave the Navy before his term was up. What a dilemma! My father had to make the choice to remain in service for His Majesty the King of Britain or follow his call from God to serve in the Congo for his King—Jesus. This was a moment of personal crisis.

He would now have to arrange an appointment with the ship's commodore and explain his reasons for asking for permanent shore leave. He decided he would spend all his shore leave the following day in prayer, up on the heather-covered hill at Scapa Flow. This he did, pleading with the Lord for this miracle to take place. When he finally met with the commodore, he told him of his call from God and his desire to serve the Lord in Central Africa. The Commodore asked only one question: "Who will supply your needs?" And my father's response was sure and fast: "My Father will."

The commodore was perfectly aware that his earthly father had passed away many years before and knew of Dad's strong Christian faith. Shortly after, on October 28, 1912, he received his "shore by purchase," having paid a nominal fee to the Navy to be discharged prior to finishing his term. This was a momentous event in his life and subsequently affected the lives of thousands of others—that story lies ahead.

From the ship in Cromarty Firth, Northeast Scotland, Dad went directly to Liverpool where his half brother, John, still lived. Liverpool was my father's home, and he always thought of it as such, even though he would only see it on three furloughs from the mission field before my family returned from the Congo in 1939.

My father spent the next year and a half orienting himself to the fact that he was no longer a sailor but a young missionary preparing for the most significant chapter of his life. This included much time spent praying and receiving advice from his church elders, his brother John, and John's wife, Margaret.

Dad's sending church in Liverpool was David Street Chapel, but after having preached widely during his Navy days in the southwest of England (including Devon and Wales), his mission was very much supported by many. He had reached a fairly high level of schooling prior to joining the service, but he was now attending Westgrove College for a few months, where he would receive special instruction. This was during 1912 and 1913. The college was located in Greenwich, London.

From there he attended the well-known Livingstone College in Leyton, which was also in the London area. This was a wonderful training centre for missionaries going to a vast number of locations around the world. He met many young missionary male and female recruits. The emphasis was on pioneering mission work in new fields, with much to learn from David Livingstone's amazing work in Central Africa. Hundreds of young men and women were financially aided by a well-known Christian named Huntingdon Stone. He paid for men's medical training, and women were given professional instruction in obstetrics.

While my dad was studying at Livingstone College, he had the opportunity to hear the illustrious Scottish missionary Fred Stanley Arnot speak about his mission work in Africa. This was a great influence on Dad in terms of his decision to go to Lubaland, one of the most primitive parts of the Belgian Congo.

Now it was off to France—not for a holiday break but for very concentrated language studies since the official language in the Belgian Congo was French. This was quite a daring and, in fact, dangerous trip to make, due to the imminent start of WWI. Dad's time in France, which equalled almost a year, included a stint in St. Nazaire, where upon presenting his British passport he was detained and taken to the sentry at a nearby French military camp. He was finally released when he volunteered to work in the hospital for some time, which he did. There couldn't have been a better place to immerse himself in the French language! After some time, Dad proved he wasn't a risk and travelled to Roanne, near Lyon, where he was warmly received by the church members he had been referred to.

Many treasured friendships were left behind when Dad returned to England. It was now 1915, and the war had commenced, but Dad made it back to Liverpool without any problems. God was watching over him for sure! He had been officially discharged from the Navy, so he was not recruited for further service in the military. He was now free to leave for his mission to the Congo.

I've attached a copy of an article about Fred Arnot from *Echoes of Service* magazine, dated September 1958. In a nutshell, this article provides the background to Dad's work in the Garenganze in Congo, following in the footsteps of Arnot and others. I have left other books about Arnot in the family archive, including Arnot's first book, *Garenganze*. The copy is a first issue, published in 1889.

Other books I'm leaving in the family archive include:

Back to the Long Grass (Dan Crawford)
Thinking Black (Dan Crawford)
Dan Crawford: Missionary and Pioneer in Central Africa (George Edwin Tilsley)
Dawn in the Dark Continent (James Stewart)
Turning the World Upside Down (W. T. Stunt)
African FootPrints: A Sixty Year Safari (Zelma Virgin)

The last title is a book about James Clarke written by his daughter. Clarke was a senior missionary with whom Mum and Dad worked from 1915 to 1920—five of the most difficult years they spent in the Congo. In this time span they had to contend with blazing heat, sickness, and frequent opposition, primarily from the chiefs. Travel in Congo was all done by foot at the time.

World War I was on the way, and it was an appropriate time for my dad to make the actual move to Africa. With the blessing and support of everyone at David Street Chapel and beyond, he set off for Garenganze, likely sailing on one of the Union-Castle ships to Cape Town. This line had been sailing to Cape Town carrying mail and passengers since 1900. The sunny, warm voyage to the Cape would be my dad's last holiday for many years. It allowed him about three weeks to reflect, make preparations, and pray.

So, the splendid river of Dad's life took a turn and flowed south to Africa. It was now 1915, and he was a single lad about to turn twenty-seven.

There must've been great excitement on the part of the passengers as Table Mountain, overlooking Cape Town, came into view. It is indeed a gorgeous approach to a beautiful town, with its white beaches, treed parks, mountain slopes, and clear blue sky. The last time that Dad had seen Cape Town was as a young sailor en route to China with the Royal Navy in 1906. What tremendous events had taken place since then—and what incredible things were yet to come under God.

The stop in Cape Town was not long but served to reunite my father with some of the Christians he had met back in 1906. There were now many who looked forward to meeting him from the Cape Town Brethren assembly, along with others from assemblies around the country. They were aware of his commendation in the UK to go to the Congo, and many became lifelong prayer partners and supporters.

My father next headed north to the Congo via the Cape-to-Cairo train, which was the brainchild of Cecil Rhodes. Rhodes' goal was to link the colonies under British rule with other countries all the way up to Egypt. The development of that rail line is a story in itself. Dad's voyage on the train was the epitome of luxury compared to what lay ahead in terms of travel, although the carriages had hard seats or bunks, and the trip was long and tedious. Still, it must have been exciting, as the train passed through the incredible scenery and places steeped in African history. The native crew was efficient and did its best to provide as much comfort to the passengers as possible, including simple meals, tea, and limited water, with fresh supplies at the major stops.

Commencing from Cape Town, the major stops were Kimberley, Johannesburg, Salisbury, Bulawayo (famous for the magnificent Victoria Falls), and Livingstone (named after Doctor David), then it was northward into the very heart of Africa. The next stop was in Elizabethville (bypassing

Bunkeya on this first trip, the seat of Chief Msiri's empire in Lubaland), and from there it was on to Bukama, the very name of this stop evoking African intrigue and adventure. This was the end of the line at the time and, indeed, the beginning of the trail. My dad's journey now began in earnest, primitive style to his destination of Luanza, where Dan Crawford had arrived to spread the gospel in 1889.

Period And Activities In Luanza

In the period between 1889 and 1915, Dan Crawford and his coworkers had established a very well-organized mission centre and contributed greatly to the development of the village of Luanza.

These courageous warriors for Christ brought Dad up to speed on much that was to follow over the next number of years, as Dad worked in fellowship with the many men and women of the Garenganze Evangelical Mission. There was, however, the whole adventure of Dad's being redirected to Kabumbulu, where he was tasked with beginning missionary work alone with the local natives in the most primitive of conditions. I use the word *alone* as he was not as yet married to my mum. His good friend Ernest Rout of New Zealand travelled with him and Clarke to this northern section of Lubaland. Rout decided to remain further south at Kiolo, while Dad continued on to Kabumbulu on his own. Clarke returned to his mission base, leaving Dad with a tent. But, of course, he always had the fellowship and support of other Brethren missionaries from time to time over the years.

Onward To England And France

After spending five years in Lubaland, Dad was certainly feeling weary and worn, as is normal for missionaries. It was time for a break and rest but also to pay a visit to the friends and churches whose faithful prayer and financial support had made all the incredible work in Africa possible. My father had made some very deep friendships that had seen him through the past five tough but glorious years.

Among Dad's loyal friends were the French believers in Roanne and Lyon, in the assemblies where Dad had spent time learning French some six years earlier. He would go visit them and, while there, brush up on his French, which he relied on almost exclusively to communicate with the natives in the Congo.

By this time, Kabumbulu had a vibrant church, a well set-up school, and reliable elders. Coworkers from the Garenganze mission entity with the Routs would attend to the numerous tasks and responsibilities in Kabumbulu while Dad was away. A great deal had already been accomplished, but there was much, much more that lay ahead, and only the Lord knew!

My dad would have said his goodbyes to all at Kabumbulu before setting off for his year away, then followed the same route back down the Lualaba to Mulongo, the centre for the Garenganze Evangelical Mission throughout Lubaland, where he stopped for fellowship and sharing. Then it was on to Bukama, followed by the long, wearisome train ride to Cape Town. There, he briefly visited some friends and churches, then it was back on the Union-Castle steamship to Southampton. This, again, would be a time of rest and reflection. Perhaps it included asking God to bring into his life a partner with whom to share his missionary work!

I have no doubt that it did. In spite of the fact that in those early years, Dad's hero, Dan Crawford, used to say, "A married man is a marred man," after spending many long years in Luanza and all over Lubaland, Crawford did, indeed, marry. I'm quite sure that Dad was ready to share his life with someone at this point, too.

It was now 1921, and my dad headed straight to Liverpool to see his dear brother, John, and his wife. He would spend much time here with John and Margaret and their girls. He would also spend time at David Street Chapel, reporting on his mission work, sharing, and preaching. The demands on him were great, since many assemblies wanted him to come and speak about his time in Congo. This was especially true in Liverpool and Devon, where there were so many supportive churches and friends.

So, the great river of my dad's life was flowing along. It was soon time to pay that visit to Roanne in France and share his stories with the Christians there whom he had previously befriended. Off he went by ferry from Dover to Calais, then by train via Paris to Roanne.

In the meantime, a young, unmarried Swiss nurse who had been in Roanne for some years was praying about her future serving God and, undoubtedly, whether God knew of a man who could join her in her missionary service.

Well, these two fine rivers originating from such different sources had both arrived in Roanne. While unknown to each other, they had both attended the same assembly and shared some of the same friends. It was now inevitable that they should meet.

Was this coincidence? Never! This is a remarkable event of two lives crossing, all for the majestic purpose and will of God!

So, yes, they did meet—never to part on earth until death. Whether they met at a church service or at the home of Madame Lezard ("Mamie" to Mum), I do not know, but it must have been something like love at first sight. This would have been in the fall of 1922. It is possible that they met through Madame Lezard, as she was very close to Mum and had met Dad back when he first went to France.

The wedding was simple, and I'm sure sublime, and followed the French custom of a civil marriage at Roanne City Hall, followed by a brief church blessing and a lovely, though unelaborate, reception at the first-class Buffet De La Gare, with Mamie and family as the hosts.

It was springtime in France, and Mum and Dad were given a honeymoon trip to Bordighera, where on arrival, the warm sun of the Mediterranean greeted them, as did the flowers—mimosa, hibiscus, oleander, and more. There, they were able to relax in the sun, stroll the café-lined streets, enjoy the Italian cuisine, and pray together about their imminent departure to Lubaland. By God's grace, my parents' union lasted through all the difficult times in the Congo, up until the day of Dad's passing in 1956 in Vancouver, with Mum joining him in heaven ten years later.

Their honeymoon was followed by a short visit to Mum's family in Geneva, where they also met with many of Mum's friends from her nursing days. Then it was a train from Geneva to Paris and then to Calais, a ferry to Dover, a train to London, and then on to Liverpool for a final round of introductions and a reception at John and Margaret's with numerous friends.

Once all the appropriate documents had been procured and travel arrangements made, Mum and Dad left for Cape Town aboard the Union-Castle ship once more. It would be a quiet three weeks in which Dad would have related to Mum some of what lay ahead. That being said, Mum was well prepared to be a full missionary partner, not just a wife. I can just see them walking the decks, chatting and singing. Perhaps they sang the following hymn in French:

> *Quel Bonheur de marcher avec Lui!*
> *Quel Bonheur de marcher avec Lui!*
> *Il Conduira tous les pas, do mon voyage ici-bas.*

I assume that Mum became pregnant on this trip since my sister, Pearl, was born on November 5, 1923. What a great way to start their life in the Congo! All three of us kids were born in the Congo—Pearl, Alf, and I, each two years apart.

After three weeks on the ship, they would've seen it: the famous landmark Table Mountain with its equally famous "tablecloth" of thin clouds welcoming all on board to Cape Town. The time they spent here would have been fairly brief, but my dad had many supporters in Cape Town who would have been thrilled to meet his new bride.

The next leg of their voyage to Kabumbulu would be a challenge, but Mum was no stranger to difficulty. Her commitment was as strong and enduring as Dad's.

Martha Wilding
(Née Vuadens)

The Lord blessed me with an incredible mother: full of faith, abounding in love for her family, and courageous as a pioneer missionary in the Congo. Early in life, with the option of a secure life in Switzerland, she chose the path of God to live a hard and strenuous life in primitive conditions.

Elsewhere in this book, I have likened my parents' lives to two great rivers flowing independently in very different circumstances. I often stood and watched the two great rivers Rhone and Arve joining and becoming one in Geneva. That is how I see my parents after they married in Roanne, France, in 1921. What a powerful river was born out of two!

Mum was born in a small lakeside community called Creux-de-Genthod, just outside of Geneva, Switzerland, on July 16, 1900.

Her father, Henri Edouard Vuadens, was from Blonay in the same canton of Vaud but was living in Genthod. I have visited Genthod two or three times and was amazed at how many tombstones in the cemetery were inscribed with the name Vuadens. I don't know that much about the Vuadens family, but as I understood from Mum, they had their origins in the French Huguenot community.

My mother's mother, Joséphone Armanda Braschbacher, was from Lautig, Prussia. As with the Vuadens, I don't know that much about my grandmother's family.

When Mum was about nine months old, her father accepted a position as an engineer in Petropolis, Brazil, near Rio. In those days, ships were in the early stages of development, and the voyage for the family of seven would have been very long and difficult. After leaving from France and crossing the Atlantic in very cramped quarters, they would have sailed down the coast of the Americas, finally reaching Rio to much relief.

Very shortly after they settled in Petropolis, problems arose with the owners of the firm my grandfather had the contract with, and he was forced to find another job. This created some difficult times, but he eventually found a position, and life in Brazil was good. My grandparents built good relations with people there, including many Catholic believers, and the family became part of the community. Henri and Joséphone were deeply committed Christians and became part of a North American Baptist mission.

How my grandparents met, I do not know, but it was possibly through a Christian connection. My grandfather had Huguenot roots in France, and possibly my grandmother had the same. My mum, Martha, was the youngest in the family. She had a sister, Lily, and three brothers, Ernest, Leopold, and Bill.

Lily married Will Holland, an Englishman, and they had two sons, Harry and Charlie. They later adopted a daughter, Flossie. We met all of our cousins, first in Switzerland, and we were reacquainted with Harry in Scotland during WWI. Harry and his wife, Edith, later moved to Vancouver and had two children, Denise and Ken.

Ernest married Anna, a Swiss-Italian living in Brazil, and they had a daughter, Nora, who became a very accomplished concert pianist in São Paulo. We never met them. Leopold married Aldaiza, a Brazilian, and they had no children. Bill remained single, eventually moving to Switzerland. I recall our family visiting him when we went to Geneva in 1939. He was working on a farm and vineyard. He passed away quite early in life. He had spent several years as a merchant seaman.

Mum became a missionary at an early age, taking time out of school to reach out to others through gospel. She often spoke about helping adults who were missionaries involved in evangelism and medical work, especially in the poor areas. Nursing was in her heart, and she volunteered in a fairly primitive hospital with people afflicted with leprosy. Studying nursing lay not too far ahead. Often, these mission visits were made on horseback, which my mum managed quite skillfully.

She often told a story of being with her brother Leopold, playing with their family dog at a nearby river that had a strong current. At one point she tripped and plunged into the turbulent river. Immediately, their dog jumped in after her and held her until her brother could haul her back to the riverbank. With Mum, there was never a dull moment!

After much prayer and consultation with her father and other believers, my mother decided to return to Geneva to study nursing. Alone, she made her way back across the Atlantic, where she enrolled in the program at the Hôpital Cantonal de Genève. This took place on August 23, 1915. Her studies went very well, and she received her nursing certificate.

On October 31, 1918, my mother became a registered nurse with the Alliance Suisse des Gardes-Malades. Thus, with the Lord's help and the encouragement of her family, my mother was now on the way to what would become the primary work of her life. While studying in Geneva, she had committed herself to the assembly her cousins attended and made many friends who continued to pray for her for many years after. She also enjoyed attending with her cousin Emily the very open evangelical church that met at the opera building near the university. The pastor there was a well-respected preacher and did much work in the cause of Christ in the city of Geneva.

World War I was just ending, and one way or another, Mum heard of the need for nurses in France to help wounded soldiers returning home from war. She went to Roanne and was recruited by the French Red Cross to visit homes as well as the hospital to attend to the needs of the injured.

These were tough and sorrowful years, but Mum's faith and vitality saw her through.

Whether she had contact with the Christians in the assembly in Roanne before going, I do not know, but it is very possible. In any event, a certain Madame Lezard took her into her heart and was like a mother to her during this time. Madame Lezard was a widow and had a daughter Mum's age. She ran the first-class Buffet De La Gare, working long hours to support her family. I believe she also had a son who had served in the French army. This relationship between my mum and Madame Lezard lasted for many years after Mum left Roanne. We, as a family, met Madame Lezard and her daughter and husband, George Brun, and their family. In later years, I would visit them whenever I happened to be passing through Geneva.

Another family that became very close with Mum were the Crouzets. There was also a family by the name of André. Apart from the time my mum spent tending to the wounded, there were times of great happiness in Roanne. Visits to Lyon were quite frequent, and she had many friends. Lyon had the reputation of having the finest cuisine in all of France! In fact, one of the most famous restaurants in the country was in Roanne— Les Trois Gros. Of course, Mum could not afford to dine here, but her dear friend Madame Lezard gave her free rein at the first-class Buffet De La Gare, where one could eat very well for a lot less!

From Mum's arrival in Roanne in 1918 until 1920, Mum was deeply involved in the care of the wounded soldiers in their homes, dressing wounds, dispensing medication from doctors, and helping out in the hospital. The Americans had set up hospital facilities, also. This nursing brought Mum into the lives of dozens of families, with whom she shared her faith—praying with them and, in many cases, reading the scripture in their homes. All of this sharing apparently stirred many in their faith but seemed to trouble one of the local Catholic priests, who made his discontent known to Mum.

She never experienced any harm, but one night as she was riding her bicycle home, she was stopped at a railway crossing by some men and warned to go easy on her missionary efforts. She never lost her trust in God, however, and was generally appreciated by everyone in town.

My mum's dedication to her healing mission, both spiritual and physical, was awe-inspiring. I can recall many of the hymns she used to sing in French throughout my childhood. Here is one:

> From Chants de Victoire: Qu'il fait bon à ton service.
> *Qu'il fait bon a ton service, Jesus mon sauveur!*
> *Qu'il est doux le sacrifice que t'offre mon coeur.*
> *Mon desire, mon voeu supreme, c'est la saintite,*
> *Rien je ne veux et je n'aime que ta volonte*
> *Travail, douleur et souffrance, non, je ne crains rien,*
> *Toi Jesus, mon esperance, voila mon seul bien.*

Mum had become a keen student of the Bible as a young girl, and now the fruit of that was that she was able to share its truths with winsomeness and authority from the Holy Spirit. As mentioned earlier, her basic duties were to work with the Red Cross and local authorities and relatives in receiving the wounded, fatigued, and displaced soldiers, mostly in their homes. But Mum never took advantage of her position, only witnessing at appropriate times and doing so with wisdom and caring. Through her respectful witnessing, the faith of many Catholics was refreshed and many nonbelievers were drawn to Christ.

Roanne was a very attractive town with its central city hall overlooking a large town square and park, with numerous fine churches and buildings. The railway station was one of those impressive structures with steel girders and glazing for the roof, and it was well-serviced by two buffets. While nearby Lyon was regarded as the gastronomical centre of France, Roanne had some fine cuisine—most notably, Les Trois Gros restaurant.

Now, the lovely river of my mother's life, flowing as it had through many places and fascinating experiences, crossed at last with my father's—and the rest, as they say, is history.

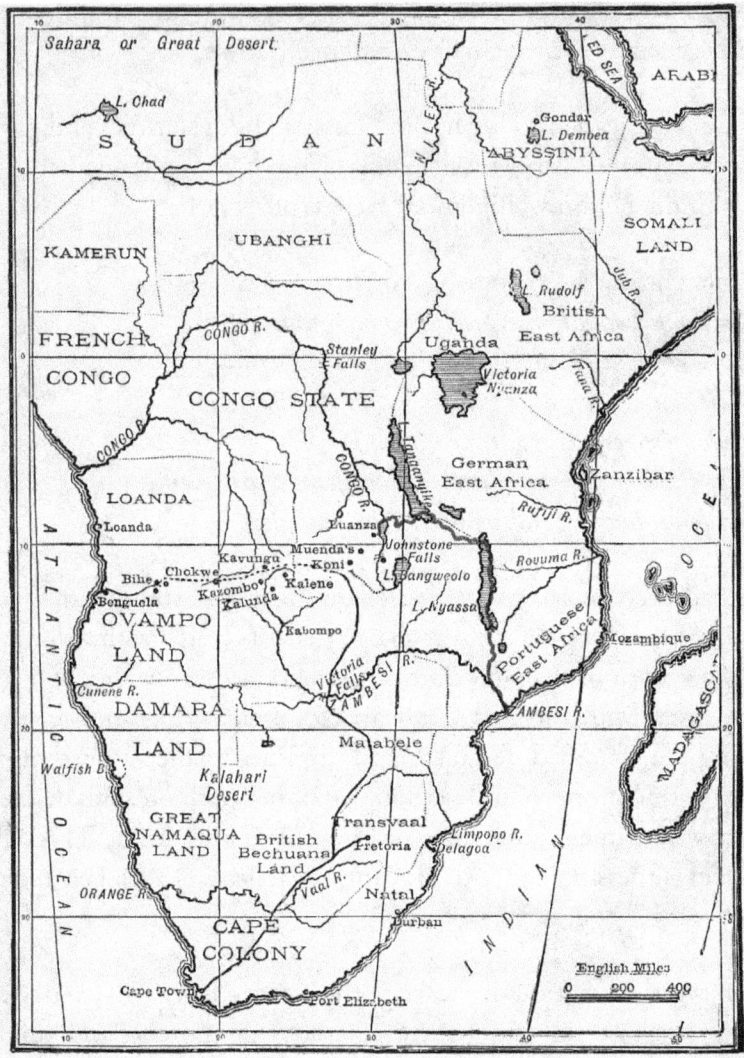

Map of Central Africa that shows the present-day Democratic Republic of Congo as Congo State, which was named Belgian Congo during the period of the events described here. The star locates Kabumbulu on the banks of the Lualaba River, the main tributary flowing northward into the mighty Congo River, eventually spilling into the Atlantic Ocean.

The map shows the European colonial states. How this all took place and what happened as a result is fascinating but will not form part of this story.

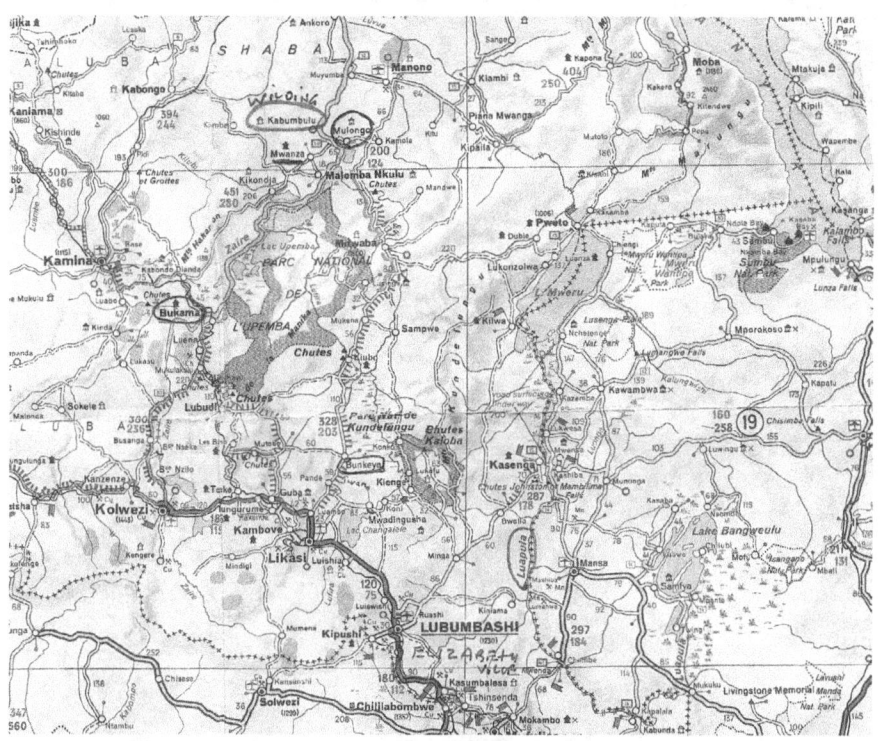

Detailed map with locations circled

This present-day map shows the general area of eastern Congo.

Pioneer missionaries

Several pioneer missionaries to Central Africa are shown in late 1800. In the front row, first and second from right, are Dan Crawford and Fred Stanley Arnot.

My dad is shown here in his Royal Navy uniform.

CERTIFICATE of the Service of Robert James Wilding in the Royal Navy.

The corner of this Certificate is to be cut off whenever it is considered that the man's antecedents and character are such as to render his re-entry at any future time undesirable. Whenever the corner is cut off the fact is to be noted in the Ledger.

Port Division	Devonport
Official Number	
Date of Birth	24th September 1888
Where born — Parish	Toxteth
Town or County	Liverpool, Lancashire
Usual place of Residence	14 Graham St, Dingle, Liverpool
Trade brought up to	Errand Boy
Religious Denomination	Church of England
Can Swim	Yes
Man's signature on discharge to pension	

Continuous Service Engagements

Date of actually volunteering	Commencement of time	Period volunteered for	Date Received	Nature of Decoration
Oct 05	27 Sept 06	12 years		

Description of Person	Stature		Colour of			Marks, Wounds, and Scars
	Feet	In.	Complexion	Hair	Eyes	
On Entry as a Boy	5	2½	Fresh	Dark Brown	Grey	Two tattooed dots on left forearm
On advancement to man's rating, or on entry under 28 years	5	5	Fresh	Dark Brown	Grey	— do —
On re-entry for C.S. or for Non-C.S. after attaining 28 years						

Royal Navy Record 1

Royal Navy Record 2

These ink on parchment documents comprise the two sections of my father's Royal Navy record. The first entry shows the date he joined in Liverpool in 1904 as a seventeen-year-old.

Dad's fellow sailors in the South Seas are pictured here.

This postcard image of a typical era warship was sent by a fellow sailor.

Livingstone College, 1913

The missionary training students at Livingstone College, London, are shown here in 1913 just before heading to all corners of the world. Dad spent one year in mission orientation here, learning everything from language to pulling teeth. He is the man with dark hair in the centre of the front row.

Welcome in Garenganze

This 1915 photograph is the oldest in this collection, showing the welcoming group in Garenganze. Many Africans had responded positively to the Christian message, and though looking very somber, they warmly welcomed my father, the new white missionary. The non-Africans in the group are Mr. Anton, Mr. Sims, and Miss Bryde.

Watercolour

This fine watercolour painting was done by well-known pioneer missionary William F. Burton. It captures the view looking across the river Lualaba to the village of Kabumbulu with two houses on the hill, which were built by my father, one for our family to live in. The other was built for guests and eventually occupied by two missionary nurses: Mary Goodsell from England and Margaret Morton (née Reeves) from Australia.

> 1912. The Crisis.
> "Shore by purchase."!
>
> 1914. France. & Language.
>   The French Captain.
> 1915. Onwards to Congo.
> Mr. & Mrs. George Sims.
> Khama's Country &
> meeting Mr. Crawford & Miss Brydle.
> etc.   Mr. James Anton
> The Camp. & journey to Koni.
>   stopped! Miss Brydle!
>   Koni.
>
> Coming of Mr. Rout.
>   The Trek North. Lufira.
>   Lualaba.
> 1917. 18. 19. 20. hard years.
>   Language learning.
>   Building stations. Kivolo
>   privation. loneliness. sickness. Kob.
>
>   Triumphs in Gospel!
> Churches founded. still going on.
>   1918 — 1956.

Father's notes on life events

One of the many handwritten notes by my father recounts the years of several special life events:

1912: The crisis—shore by purchase.

1914: France and language.

1915: Onwards to Congo Khama's country. The camp and journey to Koni. Coming of Mr. Rout. The trek North. Lufira. Lualaba.

1917, 1918, 1919, 1920: Hard years. Language learning. Building stations. Kiolo. Kabumbulu. Privation. Loneliness. Sickness. Triumphs in Gospel. Churches founded. Still going on.

My mother's grandmother and grandfather from France and Germany are shown here.

My mother's parents originally lived in Switzerland but moved to Brazil when my mum was nine months old because of her father's engineering contract.

This photograph of my mother with her father, sister, and three brothers was taken around 1914, after her mother had passed away. At age eighteen, my mum left Brazil to begin her nursing training in Switzerland, still grieving her mother's death. This loss brought her to the place of deciding to follow God's calling to do Christian missionary work.

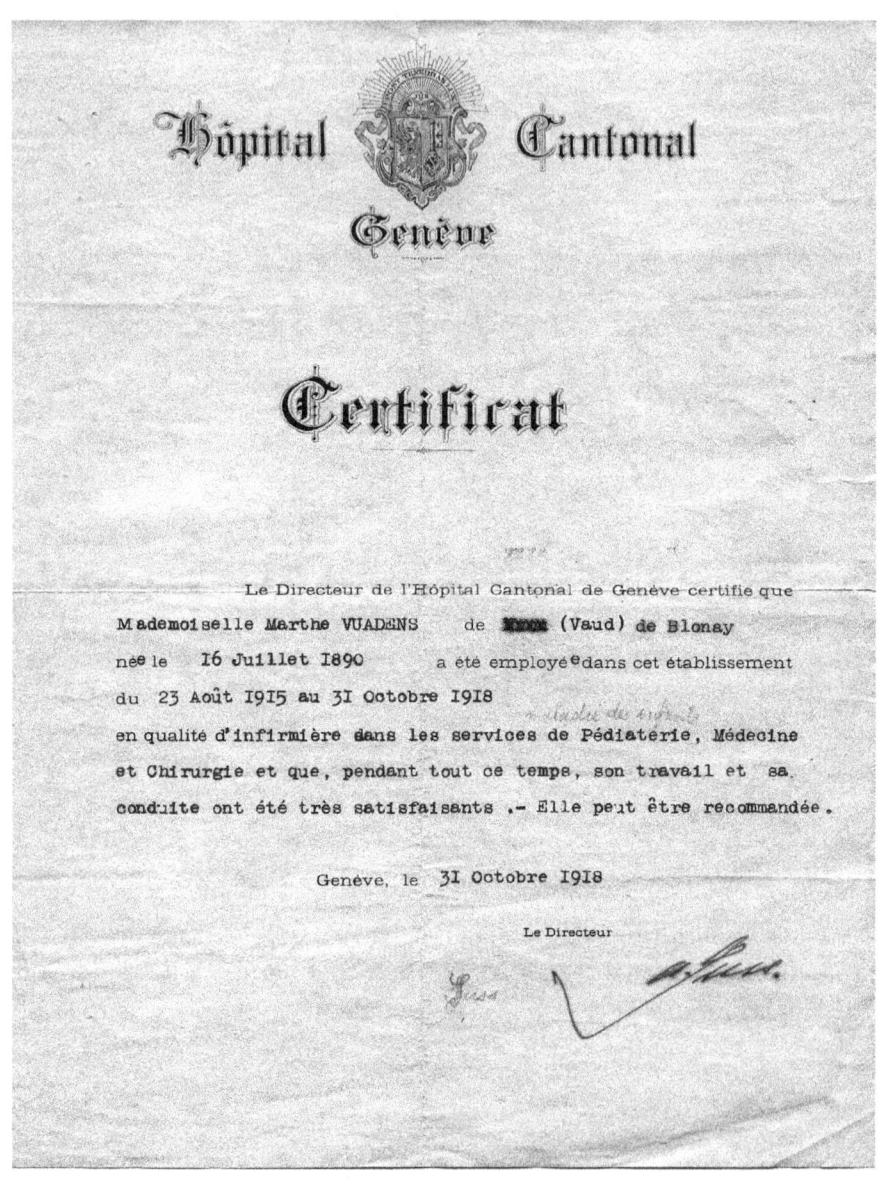

Nursing certificate

In 1918 my mother earned her nursing certificate in Geneva.

My parents

```
                                                    Registre n°  55
EXTRAIT D'ACTE DE MARIAGE                           Année      1923
        VILLE DE ROANNE (Loire)                     Folio       28

Le :   douze février              mil neuf  cent vingt trois

        A été célébré le mariage entre :
        (¹)  Robert WILDING
                        Missionnaire
né à    LIVERPOOL (Angleterre)
le     vingt sept septembre    mil huit  cent quatre vingt huit,
fils de  Charles Robert WILDING
et de    Isabella HARVEY époux décédés,
  (¹)              d'une part,
        et (¹) Martha VUADENS
                        infirmière
née à   OBNMIOD (Suisse)
le      seize juillet          mil huit  cent quatre vingt dix
fille de  Henri Edouard VUADENS
et de     Joséphine Amanda RASCHBACHER son épouse décédée,
   (²)            d'autre part.
Contrat  Néant.
Mention marginale    Néant.

                                    Pour extrait conforme
                                    Le    sept mai
                                    mil neuf cent cinquante-un
```

Marriage certificate

Here are my parents on their wedding day in 1921 in Roanne, France, and their French marriage certificate.

Mother in uniform

My mother is shown in the Congo in 1927 with her three children, proudly wearing her Swiss nursing uniform.

Chief

Chief Mushidi was known as the Tyrant of Lubaland. His life and actions had a profound influence on shaping the life of the local Africans of Central Africa, primarily among the Sangra tribe. He was in fact more than a chief, better known and remembered as a cunning and brutal despot who caused a great deal of terror, bloodshed, and suffering.

His reign as a "king" extended over a larger area than Europe, encompassing the area of Belgian Congo from eastern Lake Muere, south into Katanga, and northwest to all of Lubaland, a territory of the large Luba tribe, who were part of the numerous Sanga people.

Dad had heard much about Mushidi from the reports of Frederick Stanley Arnot and Dan Crawford in Liverpool. They had experienced firsthand the influence and efforts of Mushidi's reign of terror. It was important to understand the deeply felt concerns in the hearts of the Lubans so that Dad could relate to the people in a sensitive way. Although Mushidi had been shot and killed some time before my dad arrived in the Congo, this background information helped him to develop a clear grasp of the local situation. He also came to understand the political implications of the current Belgian rule in Congo, how it came into being, and Mushidi's efforts to retain power over this vast territory.

The life of Mushidi was one of intrigue, cunning, material gain, and power, and he achieved it all through bloodthirsty cruelty, death, shootings, and executions in his compound at Bunkeya. He was truly one of this world's awful tyrants. He would have his men spear wives and others to death and place their skulls on the posts that surrounded the compound.

From the writings of Dan Crawford and Charles Swan, as well as those of F. S. Arnot, it appears that Mushidi came to Congo from Tanganyika to trade cloth and salt for ivory, artwork, and other commodities.

Chief's wife

Dad and Mum met Mushidi's chief wife, Mahanga. She was one of 500–600 wives, through whom he controlled hundreds of villages. Each wife was assigned to a village with a gang of cruel men, answerable directly to Mushidi.

The following excerpt from *African Footprints: The Remarkable Story of John Alexander Clarke* by Zelma Virgin first introduces Mahanga in 1917. He wrote:

> June 16, 1917 Left Koni a week ago with Rout and Wilding for north. There have been recent baptisms at Koni and Bunkeya and almost weekly evidence of the Lord's presence in the salvation of souls. Camped at Dikruve River to get fresh meat. Game is now hard to get as gunpowder is freely sold to Africans. Rout had good fortune to come on a lion and lioness ten minutes from camp. Later they were able to shoot a buffalo as well. Both Wilding and Rout have made good progress in the language. Every evening we are around the blazing logs with our men.

In this book Mr. Rout explained that though normally they did not hunt lions, when suddenly confronted with a pair of them, there was not much they could do. Africans are generally not keen on eating lion meat, but the carriers were wily. Arriving at a village, they would ask some of the women to cook the "buffalo" meat and make gravy for them, and in payment for their services they would give them some fresh meat. They didn't explain that the wages would be paid in lion meat.

The account continued:

> June 21 At Kalalanombe's. There is an old man-eating lion about. He killed a woman a few days ago. Some hours downstream there is a lioness on the warpath. She jumped a barricade and seriously mauled a youth who bravely held on to her ears while friends riddled the beast with assegais. Wilding treated the young man. This evening a great crowd gathered and Mumpulu gave them a clear Gospel message. June 28 Musambei River. We are reaching people and districts that have never been visited with the Gospel. It is a joy to hear Wilding and Rout telling the story of the

Cross to Chief Msenga's people. Travelling has been very hard on our men. This hilly country has discovered the weaklings of the caravan. We are giving them a rest before descending to the Lualaba Plain. Game abounds amongst these hills. Wilding got a nice fat Zebra which wonderfully cheers our carriers. July 5 Mukanga's village. This great plain is thickly populated with large villages. We were thronged by women and children who came to see and hear us and we had many wayside chats with people. July 6 After four week's march we arrived in Mafinge's territory (Mulongo) and met his warriors on the war path in the thick of the fighting. I used all my influence but the men are so inebriated by the war spirit that it was of little use. Poor old Chief Nkomeshya- a simple old soul- cried to me for protection from Mafinge. All morning we met long lines of fleeing women and children and on reaching Nkomeshya's village found Mafinge's men plundering and sacking the whole place. I have never witnessed such a wholesale destruction. There was not a living thing left, even bananas were dragged from the trees and houses were set ablaze. I advised Mafinge to go back to his headquarters and cease attacking others. I then reported the matter to the Belgian authorities. Mafinge has heard the Gospel many times and knows about Christianity. His rule has become intolerable. However, our God is able and we trust Him to work in his heart. Rout and Wilding will settle in these parts.

The story of Mahanga is a fascinating one. At the time she is mentioned, her husband had been shot and killed by a Belgian government delegation because Mushidi refused to give up his vast and tightly controlled empire.

Wilding family

This image of the Wilding family taken from our home in front of the Lualaba River gives a picture of the remoteness and primitive conditions we lived in. Native elders required Dad to grow a beard to prove he was mature and thus an elder.

Pearl and Will

Here Pearl is seen caring for her baby brother Will, beginning a long brother–sister friendship.

Village woman

One of the faithful village women who loved to care for us kids is shown here. Note her upper body adornment, which was quite typical, as well as the ivory bracelet made from local elephant tusks.

The three kids dressed up

We three kids were "spick and span" for special occasions, always happy to be dressed in our English or sometimes French clothes.

Our family is seated in front of the verandah of our home, where the cannibals came to dance.

Three Wilding children

Here are Pearl, Alf, and Will. Through the years most of our childhood clothing came in parcels from church missionary groups and family in England via river steamer.

African play pals

From a young age we got to know our future African play pals.

Three village friends

These three village friends were great to play with and taught us many African games. They also showed us how to build small boats from papyrus.

Family with Mary Goodsell

Mary Goodsell was with the family as we passed through the small town of Livingstone, named after Scottish missionary explorer Dr. David Livingstone, who first went to Garenganze, Congo, in 1888. Reading Livingstone's journals twenty years later while serving in the Royal Navy, my father was deeply challenged to consider becoming a missionary.

Mother and Mary Goodsell off to visit villages

Among the many tasks of life in Kabumbulu, my parents regularly took time to visit some of the villages along the river. This fascinating picture shows my mother and Mary Goodsell off on a trip to a nearby village. Both were highly experienced nurses and were on the way to an outdoor grass roof clinic, taking food, medical supplies, and a homemade hammock for us kids. The carriers, strong young local men, carried the loads on poles. The number of people waiting for them in the village would only be known upon their arrival as there were many sicknesses and injuries in the area.

Older kids going to boarding schools boarding the bus

At ferry crossing

At school

Some of the older missionary kids faced long trips to go to boarding school in Sakeji. The journey involved crossing rivers and bumping over rough dirt track. There were some tears while away from home for lengthy periods. Pearl is in the centre front row of the school kids.

Building projects – forming bricks

Drying the bricks

Constructing the school

One of the very first projects on establishing a mission at Kabumbulu was building. Although the type of structure being built was totally new to the natives, they were delighted to join the paid work crews. These images give a visual picture of the brick-making process. The materials, which came from the finely erected ant hills all around, were mixed to the right consistency and poured into the molds. These were covered with branches and long grass and left in the hot sun to dry, then used to construct buildings. Progress on the walls of one of the school buildings is shown here.

Lunch break

Lunch break was followed by a short Scripture reading by my father, then everyone got back to work. On days with excessive heat and humidity, the lunch break was extended until late afternoon or evening. Most of the workers were young men who were strong and eager to increase their income. They appreciated the future use of these buildings that benefited their village.

Finished building

Numerous structures were eventually built, including a multiuse church and two houses. Many homes on the perimeters of the village were also built over the years. A bush hospital composed of numerous small huts was erected under the trees on the slope toward the village near the Lualaba.

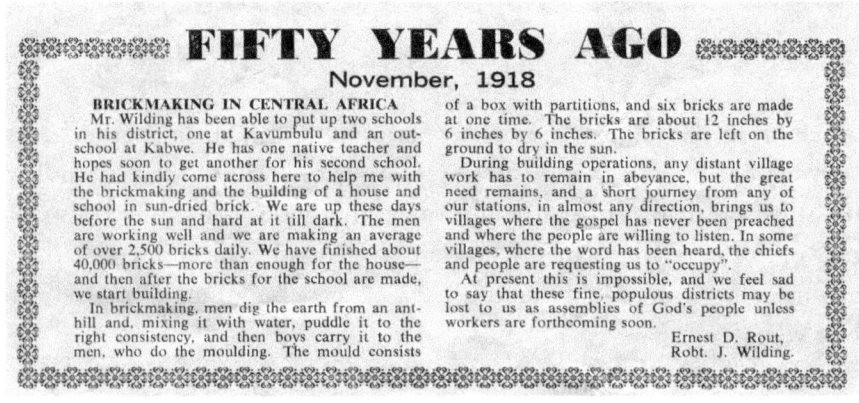

Letter to *Echoes of Service* 1918

This copy of a letter from my father and his coworker Earnest Rout was sent from Kabumbulu to *Echoes of Service* in 1918 and reprinted fifty years later in the same magazine.

Kabumbulu School

This image shows a very excited and happy crowd of school kids and some adults at Kabumbulu school. The buildings were built by Dad, and together with my mum, they began to teach the Africans how to read and write their own dialect, which until then had been exclusively oral. My parents had to learn this Kiluba dialect in order to teach it to all who came to the school, hospital, church, or on their visits. My mother is in the background leading the cheers.

Students

This 1926 image shows the bright faces of women who have gathered to learn their own dialect and study the Bible together.

Sewing class

Women were instructed on how to sew clothing for the children.

Father with students

My father is shown here with a few keen Christian believers. The ever present Lualaba River seen in the background.

Slate boards

Students, young and old, are proud of their slate boards for learning to write.

Medical work

Since there was an urgent need for medical work in the heart of primitive Congo, as an experienced nurse, my mother set herself to this task as a priority. The Belgian government supplied medications for the many ills such as malaria, blackwater fever, and other diseases. Once the Africans learned to trust the missionaries, the lines would extend far down the hillside. Word would be sent by means of the effective native drum, as shown in image 57.

Kabumbulu hospital

The Kabumbulu hospital was built on a hillside close to our house. It was designed as a village where family who brought the sick could stay, help the staff, and prepare meals. The location was chosen because of shade trees.

Out station clinic

One of the numerous outstation clinics is shown here. They were set up in villages that the natives could readily reach. Simple grass-covered shelters provided shade for patients, and nurses worked with Mum. These were very busy places when the monthly visits occurred.

Bush hospital

A view of the bush hospital is shown here, highlighting its setting.

Burn injuries

On any given day or night someone could be brought to the bush hospital my dad and his helpers built near our house on the hill. This particular man fell into the village nighttime fire in a drunken condition. Treating this type of injury was quite a challenge for my mother and the local nurses she trained. Although this man survived, his injuries had lasting effects.

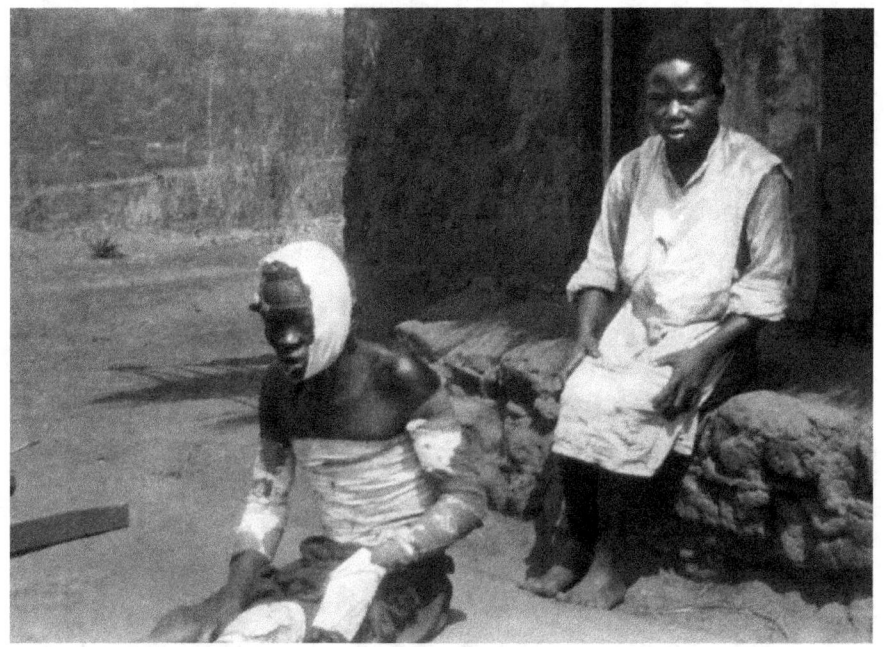

A burn patient

Here is another incident of a man falling into a fire. The Africans brewed a potent drink from roots, which often led to tragic results. Fortunately, many local women and men such as the one shown in here were well trained for these many cases.

Medical clinics

Several outstation medical clinics were set up in surrounding villages. This man made his way to the clinic on his hands and knees as he was unable to walk. These village clinics were busy places, and trained Africans were able to help run them.

Man from cannibal tribe

One day, among the other numerous patients at Kabumbulu, was this man, who belonged to the small cannibal tribe located about one kilometer away. The cause of his condition was never known.

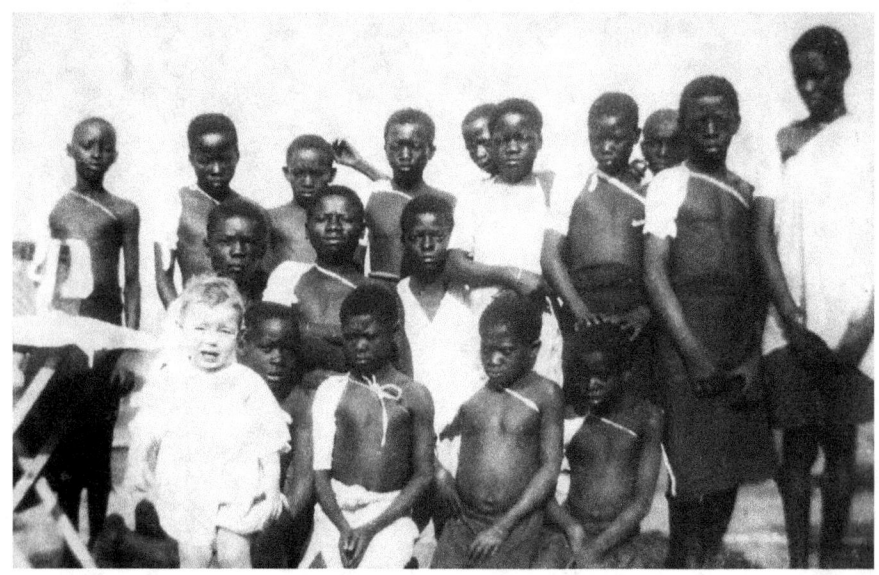

Vaccination time

Most of this group have had their shots for some condition spreading in the area. The boy behind Alf nervously awaits his turn.

Dedicated nurses

These three brave and dedicated nurses are Margaret Reeves from Australia on the left, Mary Goodsell from England on the right, and my mother seated holding my brother Alf with Pearl looking on.

Male nurses

Here are a group of trained male nurses with a young assistant.

Missionary get together

Occasionally several missionaries working with Garenganze Evangelical Mission gathered together. These infrequent visits were most uplifting and useful because of the isolation from living in different villages.

Manioc harvest

Women are seen here digging up manioc stems and roots, which provided the staple food, normally eaten outdoors in the community.

Group of women and children with one woman
carrying branches on top of her head

This group of woman and children are carrying home the freshly harvested manioc to cook.

Group of kids eating from bowl

At dinnertime meat or fish were cooked in one pot, and mush from manioc was cooked separately in another. With many fingers reaching for the food at once, each one received the same amount, as was the custom in the village. The mothers took turns cooking.

Fishing baskets

There was always an abundance of edible fish in the Lualaba River, and the villagers took full advantage of this. These images show the style of fishing baskets the women and the men used. Women placed their baskets at the edge of the river and caught many small fish. The men would plunge their round baskets into somewhat deeper water from canoes. Fish was a major part of the African diet and one of the reasons that so many villages were situated along the banks of rivers. One stark reality was the abundance of crocodiles too, so a constant vigil had to be kept.

Elder and Mission drummer

Jacoba was a faithful elder and the mission drummer, who over the years drummed hundreds of messages regarding school, church, hospital, and other local news. These messages could be heard far afield and were then passed on by other drummers.

Baptisms

While my missionary parents were kept busy with building, teaching, and medical work, the purpose of sharing the Gospel and establishing an evangelical community was also being fulfilled. Having made sure no crocodiles were around, using canoes and spears, the Christian baptism by immersion proceeded, accompanied by heartfelt native singing.

Mothers gave their babies fast baths because of possible crocodiles in the nearby water. No doubt a friend was close by watching.

Luban bridal party

This beautiful young Luban woman is a bride on her way with her family and close friends to the nearby village to meet her groom. They would have a simple exchange of their loyalty to each other, with parents sharing support of their marriage. She would then present him with the spear as a symbol of his authority, guardianship, and love. The baskets seen on all the villagers' heads contain food and gifts for the bride's family and the feast that would follow in the village.

Pearl & Alf with a grandmother

Pearl and Alf are shown with a grandmother feeding her grandchild while the child's mother was out working in the manioc fields.

the Lofoi had gone through another part of it when searching for a site before settling in Chipungu. All these men found a warm welcome in many places of this vast area and were greatly burdened about it. The door was wide open, but it was nearly 20 years later before anyone entered it!

1911, Mulongo

John Clarke paid a brief visit to villages on the Lualaba river in about 1910. But it was not until 1911 that Zentler branched out from Koni Hill to settle at Mulongo's village on Lake Kavamba, one of a chain of lakes on the Lualaba river. There was a large population there and much fish in the river and lake. Unfortunately Zentler was interned on the outbreak of World War I and on his release was not allowed to return to Mulongo and so went back to Koni Hill.

Clarke then settled in Mulongo in 1920. He took with him a number of Christians from Koni Hill and these formed the backbone of the first assembly. Like Crawford, he was a good linguist and spent much time on translating the Bible. Medical work was carried on from the beginning and especially maternity work. Mary Goodsell, S.R.N., who had gone out from Westcliff and Ashford in 1930 to Kabumbulu, moved to Mulongo in 1940.

Dr. and Mrs. Allen from U.S.A. went there in 1951 and Dr. Ray Williams, who was commended for service there from Dublin, in 1958 (not to be confused with Ray Williams from Australia who earlier had gone to North Lubaland). With the arrival of doctors the medical work increased enormously. There was, too, a certain amount of educational work, although never on such a scale as many of the Africans would have liked.

1917, Kiolo and Kabumbulu

In 1917 Rout and Wilding set out from Koni Hill with their carriers, some of whom were Christians, to find out where the Lord would have them settle. Rout decided upon Nkomeshya, later known as Kiolo, farther north down the Lufira valley, but Wilding pushed on past Mulongo to Kabumbulu, the other side of the river.

Kiolo became noted for its school work and also for the remarkable knowledge of the Scriptures possessed by the young men from the assemblies there and round about. Traders and others requiring hard-working young men of integrity would send to Kiolo from comparatively long distances to try to recruit them from there. At Lubumbashi in 1920 Rout married Irene Gresham,

424

from Invercargill, New Zealand. A number of workers went to Kiolo for language study and acclimatising before branching out elsewhere, including Mr. and Mrs. Spargo from Devon and Liverpool assemblies in 1923, Frank Brierley from New Zealand in 1924 and H. W. Beckett from New Zealand in 1932. Then, too, the Routs had the joy of welcoming their eldest son, Francis, and later his wife, as fellow-workers after their commendations from New Zealand, in 1945 and 1948.

Kabumbulu became noted for a large bush hospital. It was commenced by Dr. Julyan Hoyte, who had gone to help Wilding in 1926. Dr. George McDonald from Bray, Ireland, and Mary Goodsell, a trained nurse, joined them in 1930 and Mildred McLachlan from U.S.A. in 1934. The last named came from a well-known missionary family, the late Mr. Richard McLachlan being the editor of the missionary magazine, *Voices of the Vineyard* for many years.

1923, Muyumba

In 1923 Thomas Rolls, commended from Sydney for Luba-land in 1922, opened up work at Muyumba, still farther north from Kabumbulu, but on the east bank of the river. James Proudfoot and his wife joined him from Liverpool in 1923 and 1924 respectively, and Richard and David Howell from Australia in 1929. Jim Nock and his wife (née Gwen Leech) went there from Kalemie in 1936. They greatly expanded the work in the district during the 20 years they were there from 1936; in 1956 they went to Likasi. Albert Nock went out from West Mersea in 1938 to Muyumba, moving to Kiambi in 1953. He was fluent in French, Flemish, Swahili and Kiluba.

1924, Katwevwe

In 1924 Hoyte went from Bunkeya to Katwevwe in a fresh area about 50 miles west of Pweto, or Chamfubu. In this venture he was joined by Charles Nightingale, who had been commended from Wallasey in 1921 to serve the Lord while earning his living at Lubumbashi. After Nightingale had had two attacks of blackwater fever, Hoyte advised him to return to England for a time; this he did, returning later elsewhere. After two years of effort at Katwevwe, Hoyte felt it best to go to help Wilding at Kabumbulu.

1925, Kamubangwa

Lawrence Burrows went from London in 1923 to Mulongo. From there he visited Kamubangwa, far to the north and on the

425

Letters to Echoes of Service

Here is a copy of letters written to *Echoes of Service* in the UK. One was written in 1917 and the second in 1924 giving reports of Wilding's activity.

Chief Mufinge

Chief Mufinge is shown here with one of his several wives. He was very proud of his medal from the Belgian government recognizing him for being a good chief. He was very friendly to my parents!

Luban chiefs and pet lions

Luban chiefs loved their animals, and here one is playing with his lion cubs. In a short time, they would be let loose in the foothills behind our house.

Medicine man healing dance

The medicine man gathered the sick and other villagers, then performed his healing rituals. The chants, dance, and erection of spirit *bambuji* were all necessary parts of the healing ceremony.

Village with upright sticks

Traditional African healing herbs and leaves were given to the sick to apply to their bodies. The medicine men would then expect some gifts of food in return.

Cannibal tribe: group of women

Group of men

Two local men

A group of Cannibals with their wives paying a friendly visit.

Mixed group

Two boys

Soon after my dad arrived at Kabumbulu in 1917, he initiated contact with the cannibal tribe that lived about one kilometer from our home, establishing a relatively friendly relationship with the chief and villagers, who occasionally came to visit to sing and dance.

In one letter to *Echoes of Service* he recounted his visit to the village of the cannibals. As he entered, the chief appeared with a young man. He told my dad that the young fellow had committed something very wrong and that he was going to be killed and eaten, but since he, Bwana Kamamano, had arrived, the lad would not perish. My father was honoured to be named after Kamamano, the highest hill near Kabumbulu, visible in the watercolour image of the area.

River steamer

The river steamer returned downriver to the coastal capital of Leopoldville, a long distance with no tight schedule.

Smaller freight boats

At times the steamer would have the assistance of a smaller craft to carry excess goods going to the far interior. This is a very rare photo of the steamer.

Waiting for the river steamer

The villagers here were arriving to see the long-awaited steamer pull into the landing, bringing a variety of items to sell to passengers, most of whom would be glad to buy some bananas or papaya. The cooks on board would be after fish and any meat such as antelope and vegetables. The stop was normally brief, and with a mighty blast, the ship moved off to enthusiastic cheers from the crowd.

James Clarke leaving

This boat was named *J.C.* after its owner, James Clarke, a veteran missionary with Garenganze Evangelical Mission. It was left to my father when James Clarke retired, and in spite of the limited and expensive fuel supply, it was used extensively.

Water taxis

Many trips were taken over the years on these water taxis. They were solid and swift-moving as an equal number of Africans on either side rowed and sang their way on the Lualaba. Hippos and crocodiles were always around, but a keen watch was kept. The Wildings sheltered from the heat under the canvas.

The family here was dressed up and awaiting pickup to visit other missionaries in the area by boat.

Luban canoe

The skillful carving of a typical Luban canoe is pictured here, with an equally skillful young boy.

Village scene – Hippo hunting

Canoes were used to hunt hippos for their meat, then the catches would be towed to the bank and prepared for several villages to enjoy for many dinners.

Hippo heads

The nonedible heads were left for vultures and other animals, and the leftovers were buried.

Elephant

African elephants were not a friendly species in Lubaland. They traveled in small numbers, marauding villages looking for food and tramping over any planted vegetable or corn fields, leaving a total waste. The locals sold the ivory to three traders who were located nearby, Justus, Taschek, and Cabalio, who often visited us and shared the many stories of the trading world. They carried on a very profitable business, exchanging the ivory for such items as salt and clothing.

This king of the wildlife world used to raid my father's goat pen, a simple square of heavy wood posts about five feet high. The goats were the source of our milk all through the years. The lion would come at night, jump over into the midst of the goats, grab one in its tough teeth, and jump back over and run away. This happened too often, so Dad with his rifle and two Africans with their spears decided to wait in the pen to get the lion. This was not easy, as the lion smelled the humans in the pen, retreated around our house, then walked along our open verandah, casually looking through the mosquito net windows where Mum and we kids were sleeping. As always, a candle was burning, and the moving flame frightened the beast away in the direction of the village. Realizing the danger to the villagers, Dad and his assistants went after the lion and shot it.

Snake on stick

Snakes! There were many varieties all over the region, and several of the daily patients at the mission hospital needed urgent treatment from snake bites.

Young Lions

Young lions attacking villagers were caught by natives. They did not eat lion flesh but killed them when necessary to preserve their lives.

Crocodile

This crocodile from the river was captured by a group of men who made up an anti-crocodile and -lion squad. Notice the same man was present in both the lion and crocodile photos.

Village huts

Here is an African village typical of thousands of others across Lubaland.

Open tent

My mother and sister are seen here with a helper doing medical work in a far-off village.

Missionary families

This image captured one of those very precious times when the loneliness of life was broken by the arrival of other missionaries and their families for a few days, to fellowship and confer on mission work in that part of central Africa. These were times of sharing the tough times and the joyous times, with games, singing, and meals together, as well as introductions to the Kabumbulu villagers. My father was holding my brother Alf at the rear right, and Mary Goodsell had her hand on my head, no doubt telling me to look at Mum taking the picture.

Group of kids

Here is the gathering of what are commonly known as MKs—missionary kids.

Family picnic by water

A quiet picnic at the Lualaba River followed a busy day of activity.

Travel carriage

We travelled to villages to visit friends and play songs in the old wind-up gramophone, much to the bewilderment and delight of the village people.

In 1931 after our year-long furlough, we stopped briefly in Madeira on the way back to Kabumbulu.

Page 5 & 6 of VOC:

acquire - yata & ata
attend - jumuwa
awake = to be - pu tala   he is awake u talanga.
awake v.t. bukukija.
  " v.i. (na) buka.
back fillets = mitanda ya nyuma
backslide . pondoka .
bad manners . buendalavu .
bag   mutakoma - & mukolo
bale + kwesa
bale of mat: kivungo
bank - lukungo. (mutamba & bukila)?
barbel ? I think is mpondo ?
Bark to v.t. pobola
Barren numba - of goat kikelele.
  kole n. (not ngo)
hedge mwikulu   PAGE 6
bath v.i. = iapika   to put out to air   anika v.t.
basket = kilala (not lunyungo = sieve)
bathroom = Kyoilo .
beast . nyema
beat . ku kupila (u kupila is beat him
begin - shikula (not djilala) not tenteka,
                                          to pile up
     bandy legged . mateya ✓

Page 7 of voc:

betray = sokola (vulakanya (more deny)
better also djimbila — taka
bewitch. loa no w.
bible mukanda (is good luba)
bicycle kalete e ending
bisect chiba pabukata
blade of wheat = museke is one grain
blood issue muyeye.
strike V.T. ku kupila
trumpet V.T. ila noun mpungi
boa cons: nandolo ñ
board lubau.
boast ianya ichikuka lit (admire oneself)
bog. ntoto
boiling water mema masaluke.
bolster musamo o ending.
book. mukanda.
boy kasampe.
branch = twig, tunyala.
brave – mpikwa moyo, no n, it is broken
break V.T chimuna V.I. ladika kya ladika
of day kwe no m.
luck ngema.
bullet lufolo, kidjanga.
bundle. kipukutu
" of grass + bamboo kita
" thing nkata.

Developing a written language was an immediate challenge for those penetrating central Africa where the dialects of the tribes were solely oral. This image shows the beginnings of the vocabulary, which was the first step in writing the dialect. The schools built and operated by my parents and the African helpers they trained were used to teach the Africans how to read and write in their own language.

Eventually, the vast work of translating parts of the Bible was undertaken by my father with John Clarke and a team of Africans. This translation work started in 1917 when he established a mission in Kabumbulu, as referenced in the book on Clarke by Zelma Virgin titled *African Footprints*. This book also refers to Robert Wilding assisting in Old Testament translation. My father spent many years on this work, and after we moved to South Africa, he returned for a year to complete the first five books of the Old Testament.

The book *Turning the World Upside Down* by *Echoes of Service* records Clarke and Wilding completing this section of the Bible on page 610. The hand-printed document shows the beginnings of an alphabet in Kiluba.

My father's sermon notes in the Kiluba dialect are shown here.

1904. ... Welsh revival.
Evan Roberts.
Conversion. 1 Christening.
2 Confirmation.
3 Communion.
4 Church attendance.

1905. Royal Navy. HMS Boscawen
Portland.
prayer "say one for me."

1906. Journey to China
reading. Livingstone's of: journals.
Sept: Hong Kong — China.
Typhoon. the prayer mtg.
in Canning Town.
my call & consecration.

1906. Sydney N.S.W. Loyalty
1907. The South Seas. New Hebrides
N. Caledonia.
× "Cyrenanga". Fiji's
{Williams martyr in the Solomons. etc.
{J.G. Paton. the S. Seas.
× Mr Jarlsng of New Caledonia!
the call emphasised!
1908. Still in South Seas. etc.
1909. Home ... Home Fleet.
... abrahams saved!

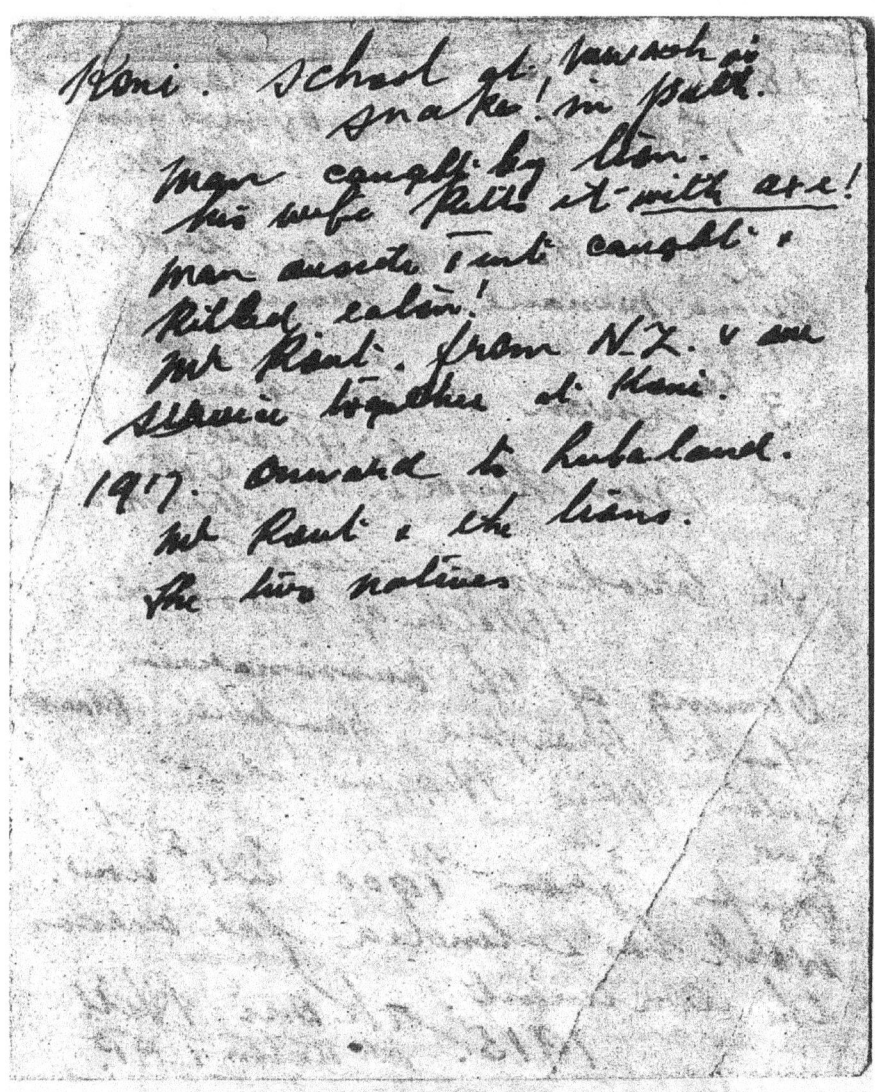

These personal notes by my dad provide the dates of major events.

> Mision
> Kabumbulu.
> 16-12-50
>
> Kudi Bwana R.J. Wilding
> Bwana Kamamonyo.
>
> Natume uno mukada obe wa lwimu tu ba kwimuna lwimu ludumudi Mfumwetu Jesu Kidishitu. Tu baimuna ndona ne bana ba Mangaleta ne Joni ne Willi Kabange Mata we mwimuna.
> Tu baimuna bene Kidistu bonso.
>
> mwamo Umbulaya.
>
> Lelo kashia mwenda kwituvuka mpika batwe tu bemu vuluka ne Goano Ilunga mwine Bauzambuyu we mwimuna. Le mwaiswene ne wami mwana (Levi Ilunga) wa fwile † Umwaka wa 19-4-48. Emevafwile (Levi), pano ngidi ne bana basamba (6) pa buntu lwa Leza kuno kwetu ku Kabumbulu bene Kidistu badiko banji. Kadi Tu pwilanga Sukola miyu le dya Jenga. ne bene Kidistu kuno abe mwimuna.
> Lalaipo.
>
> Ami Yakoba Ngobla

This letter was written many years later to my parents from Jacoba, a faithful elder and the official drummer of the speaking drum.

About the Book

Will Wilding recounts the story of his parents and their three young children living in the Belgian Congo between 1914 and 1935. His father, Robert Wilding, left his job as a seaman in the British Royal Navy to begin his work as a missionary while he was still single. He was left alone with a tent in Lubaland, one of the most primitive areas of the region. During a year away, he met and married a young Swiss nurse, Martha Vuadens, and after a brief honeymoon she joined the work in Kabumbulu.

This book tracks the lives of Will's family as his parents worked with the local Luban tribe, leading building projects, setting up bush hospitals and medical clinics, training local assistants, creating a written language, starting churches, and translating parts of the Bible. They built warm relationships with the surrounding tribes, including the nearby cannibals. The book is illustrated with historic photos of the wildlife and interactions with the local people.

About the Author

Robert William Wilding is a retired architect with a forty-year practice in Vancouver, Canada. Born at a mission station in Lubaland, Will spent his first eight years in Kabumbulu before moving to Cape Town, South Africa, for further education. Of the three children, Will was the keeper of his family's documents and photos. Throughout his life Will held his parents in high esteem and viewed them as heroes. Will completed his architectural studies in Glasgow and received several awards and heritage designations. His parents' example and prayers deeply influenced Will's own life of service, and he is thrilled to fulfill his dream of honouring his parents' lives by sharing this remarkable story.

www.ingramcontent.com/pod-product-compliance
Lightning Source LLC
LaVergne TN
LVHW011720060526
838200LV00051B/2978